Angus's thoughts were interrupted as Uncle Ivan burst into the kitchen.

"Good morning, me hearties!" he bellowed, swaggering like a sea captain.

Uncle Ivan's face was lit by a beaming smile, but Angus looked at his uncle's beard. Clinging to the straggly strands were the tell-tale signs of chocolate milk. Angus couldn't wait to hear his explanation.

"So, Uncle Ivan," started Angus, playing along with the prank. "I couldn't find my chocolate milk in the fridge."

His uncle grinned. "Is *that* what it was?" he answered. "That's mighty tasty milk!"

Uncle Ivan patted Angus on the shoulder. "That reminds me of the worst milk I have ever tasted. Did I ever tell you about the time I was marooned on a Zanzibar beach with some lions?"

The children nodded, but their uncle just carried on.

"All I had to drink was lion's milk. Luckily, a passing Chinese junk rescued me, but on board that junk, there was nothing to eat but barbecued snakes!"

Uncle Ivan

Class Number	Bar Code Number

MAYO COUNTY LIBRARY

The latest date entered below is the date by which this book should be returned. It must be returned to the Branch Library from which it was borrowed. It may be renewed (twice only) if not required by another reader. When renewing by telephone, please quote the Bar Code Number above. Fines are charged on overdue books and readers are accountable for any books they lose or damage.

Angus, Bailey and Connor

Some wildlife Park animals

...hews to use their
...gerated tales of
...they begin
...loits
...*Heroic*

Exaggerated Unlikely Exploits

"Who drank the last of my chocolate milk?" growled Angus.

Angus *knew* who had drunk his chocolate milk. But he grumbled to Connor, his brother, and Bailey, his sister, anyway. It had to be Uncle Ivan! He loved being a prankster — that was why the three siblings secretly loved staying at his house.

Angus remembered what his mother told Uncle Ivan as she dropped them off for the weekend.

"Have fun, Ivan," their mother had said. "But don't exaggerate your exploits. After last weekend, their teachers were shocked by their exaggerated stories!"

"Yuck!" screamed his niece and nephews.

Uncle Ivan was a great storyteller. And it was cool to imagine their uncle marooned with lions and drinking their milk.

"Ah, milk," remembered Uncle Ivan. He opened the fridge. There were clinking and clanging sounds as their uncle pushed bowls and bottles around. Finally, he pulled out an unopened bottle of chocolate milk for Angus.

"There you go," he winked. "Just kidding!"

Just as Angus had predicted, he *was* part of Uncle Ivan's first prank for the day. Over breakfast their uncle proceeded to tell another tale.

"After the Chinese junk rescued me, I was invited to the castle of Zortan, a rich emperor in China," said Uncle Ivan. "He could see I was hungry so we had *yum cha*. And some of the foods were still moving," he chuckled.

"Yuck!" screeched the three siblings.

"Then Zortan wanted me to try something that looked like big buffalo eyes! I pretended to love the taste, but to be honest I just felt ill!"

"No way!" groaned the children. After that most unlikely exploit, they all felt ill, too.

Uncle Ivan found a bowl of mushy peas for breakfast, and ate them far too quickly. He burped and belched and then beamed at the children.

"Whoops, excuse me!" he said. "Those peas reminded me of animal droppings. I say! Would you like to visit the wildlife park today?" he suggested.

"Yes, please, Uncle Ivan!" said Angus, Bailey and Connor.

"That reminds me," smiled Uncle Ivan. "Last time I went to the zoo, the ticket lady asked me to remove my big furry coat. She said I might be mistaken for a grizzly bear! Can you imagine that?"

"Did I tell you about the time ... " said Uncle Ivan, looking backwards.

"Watch the road!" screamed out Angus from the front seat. He *was* watching the road and Uncle Ivan's driving was more than a little scary!

"Quite right, co-pilot!" said Uncle Ivan. "Talking about co-pilots, that reminds me of the time I helped pilots land a plane on an icy runway."

The children rolled their eyes,

"Okay, now imagine you're in Siberia," he began in a haunting voice. "That's in Russia. It was freezing cold, minus 50 degrees Celsius.

"The runway's lines and lights were covered in snow. I had to mark out the runway to show the pilots where to land.

"I wasn't sure how I was going to do that. But just then, ten Siberian tigers stopped to help me mark out the runway. And the plane landed safely."

Bailey and Connor clapped at their uncle's story. Angus just kept his eyes on the road.

Finally, they arrived at the wildlife park. Uncle Ivan and the three kids scrambled out of the car.

As soon as Uncle Ivan had led the way into the wildlife park, his stories began again.

"Kangaroo grunts," he whispered, following the sounds towards the kangaroo enclosure. "Reminds me of my time as a kangaroo jockey in the outback of Australia!

"I was in the town of Boolydooly for the kangaroo races. My first race was against another tough jockey, Mad Butcher-Bill Baggins," continued Uncle Ivan. "I swung myself up onto my big, fierce red kangaroo and held onto his ears.

"In a flash, we were off!" he said excitedly.

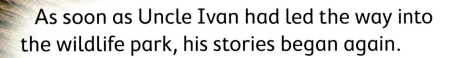

Angus saw a kangaroo head pop up from inside the enclosure. Could it be listening?

"At full hop, Mad Butcher-Bill swerved in front of us and we almost collided," recounted Uncle Ivan. "Well, *my* big red didn't like that at all! With a secret command from your Uncle Ivan, he bounded out in front and walloped Mad Butcher-Bill right in the nose with his paw. That Mad Butcher-Bill was so surprised he fell right off."

Uncle Ivan smiled.

"My big red kangaroo went on to win that race — and all the others that day!"

Suddenly, Angus saw the kangaroo jump up and down as if it was trying to get Uncle Ivan's attention. Maybe it *was* listening, after all!

"Look!" said Angus, pointing at the kangaroo.

The kangaroo thumped the ground with its tail. Slowly, one by one, a row of kangaroo heads popped up from around the enclosure.

Uncle Ivan made a clicking sound and even more curious kangaroos appeared. Within moments, the front of the enclosure was lined with hopping kangaroos, staring at Uncle Ivan. They clicked and chattered in excitement.

"They've heard this story before," winked Uncle Ivan. He waved cheerily at the kangaroos. "Nice to see you all again."

"Nice to see you, too," clicked the two big red kangaroos.

CAUTION

Chapter 3

UNLIKELY EXPLOIT AHEAD

Did He Really Save the Grizzly Bears?

"Grizzly bears!" declared Uncle Ivan, sniffing the air mysteriously.

"And they remind you of … ?" asked Connor.

"My time in the Yukon, of course!" said Uncle Ivan, hurrying towards the bear enclosure. "When I saved a family of grizzly bears!"

Uncle Ivan began telling his next exploit the moment the children caught up with him.

"One winter, it was so cold that animals everywhere hibernated for an extra month. The snowfalls were so heavy that by the time you put your foot back on the ground to take your next step, the falling snow had covered your footprint completely!"

13

"One morning, I went out to check my letterbox. It was at the end of our road so the postie didn't have to travel along it — it could be dangerous sometimes," said Uncle Ivan. "But I got lost, because the log cabin I'd built out of tree trunks had disappeared. Completely covered in snow!"

Suddenly the grizzly bears' grunts and snores stopped. The children were puzzled by the silence.

"Well, there was nothing else to do but to try and find some shelter," he carried on. "Eventually, I found a nice warm cave, and headed inside. Imagine my surprise when I stood on what felt like a piece of thick, warm carpet!"

Bailey wrinkled her forehead. Surely this was too much of an exaggeration, even for her uncle. And all this talk of ice and snow had made Connor think of something else.

Ice-cream.

"Of course, it wasn't carpet," chuckled Uncle Ivan. "It was fur. Imagine my surprise when I found myself staring into three pairs of grizzly bear eyes!"

"But just as I was about to scarper out of there, I heard a terrible commotion at the cave entrance."

"An angry male grizzly bear was trying to get in. Well, there was only one thing to do," Uncle Ivan said. "I had to scare off the ferocious bear. With one deep breath, I leapt up and … "

Uncle Ivan let out a deep, rumbling roar. In the bear enclosure in front of him, a huge lumbering grizzly bear stood up. Uncle Ivan waved politely, and carried on with his tale.

"The male grizzly was so surprised, he shot backwards out of the cave and into a tree. The force of the impact knocked about a tonne of snow off the branches and SPLAT! It covered the surprised grizzly like an enormous frozen seagull dropping!"

Angus, Bailey and Connor laughed.
Then they heard another deep, rumbling roar.
But this time it wasn't their uncle.

Three bears had appeared. They stared at
Uncle Ivan. One of the bears roared again.

Uncle Ivan
roared in reply.
For a moment,
it seemed like
they were having
a roaring bear
conversation.

Then Uncle Ivan waved goodbye. He cupped
a hand around his ear.

"Ah!" said Uncle Ivan excitedly, as he hurried
towards the next enclosure. "I know those
howling sounds. I remember them from the
time I accidentally parachuted into a forest
and tamed a pack of wolves!"

"My parachute really came in handy," said Uncle Ivan.

"Sounds dangerous! Why were you parachuting?" asked Bailey, as they all arrived at the wolf enclosure.

"Well ... imagine this. We were flying over a huge forest in Canada and I jumped out to land in a nearby field. But the strong winds pushed me back towards the forest — and towards a pack of hungry wolves."

"And you tamed them?" asked Angus.

"Sure did. Even though I was dangling from my parachute, I still managed to tame them."

"I was caught up in the branches of a massive maple tree when I felt myself slipping. I looked down into wolf mouths dribbling with saliva. I was in *big* trouble!" Uncle Ivan explained.

As Uncle Ivan told his story, wolf after wolf appeared from their dens, howling loudly!

"A pack of starving wolves circled below me, licking their chops and howling," breathed Uncle Ivan, his eyes widening. "My parachute slipped again and I sagged lower.

"The wolves were leaping up, nipping at my ankles. Quickly, I felt through my pockets — and found something that saved my life. Can you guess what that was?"

"No," the children answered breathlessly. "Tell us!"

"Corn-snack squiggles!" hooted Uncle Ivan. "Wolves love 'em, you know! So after I crashed down on top of what felt like a thick, soft fur rug – although a little lumpy – I tore open a packet. As quickly as I tipped them into my hands, those wolves were gobbling them up! We became the best of friends."

"I've never heard of wolves making friends with humans *or* eating corn-snack squiggles," said Connor, with a sceptical frown.

Uncle Ivan raised his eyebrows. "Well, let's see about that!" he said, reaching into his pocket and pulling out a half-eaten packet of squiggles.

"No, Uncle Ivan!" protested Bailey. "You can't feed corn-snack squiggles to the wolves! It's against the rules — you can't feed the animals."

"You're right, dear," he replied. "Although they look like they're keen to gobble them up."

"So we'll never know," piped up Angus.

"Never know what?" asked Uncle Ivan.

"Whether or not this unlikely exploit is *actually* true," replied Angus.

Uncle Ivan shrugged his shoulders.

"Well, I *was* the only human there," he admitted. "So, it's difficult to *prove* that what I'm telling you is the truth."

"Hmm," murmured Angus, who knew there was no way he would ever find out. And it didn't really matter because he just loved hearing the stories anyway.

Then something odd happened.

Slowly, one by one, all the nearby animals gathered behind Uncle Ivan.

"Well you may not know if my stories *are* true," said Uncle Ivan. "But they sure do ignite your imaginations, don't they?"

"Not only ours," added Angus, nudging Bailey and Connor.

"Turn around!" they shouted together.

Uncle Ivan turned around, and waved to the animals that had crowded along the fence. And what happened next would have almost deafened every visitor at the wildlife park.

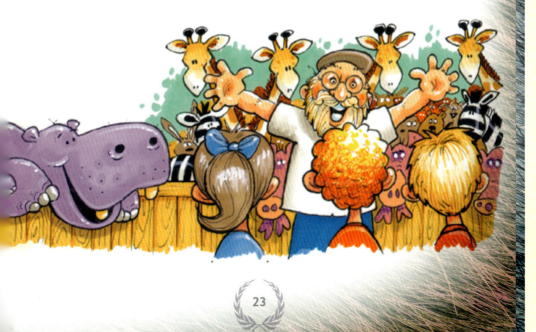

Without warning, the gathering of animals erupted into an explosion of shrieks and grunts and hoots and squeaks and cries and screams and roars.

And, for one uncertain, curious, far-fetched moment, the noise from the animals seemed wilder than any of Uncle Ivan's stories of unlikely exploits.